SMOOTHIE TIME

HEALTH, NUTRITION AND HOME ECONOMICS

HOMESCHOOLING CURRICULUM & COOKBOOK

Linda Janisse & Julia Stockman

This Book Belongs to:

NAME:

DATE:

AGE:

GRADE:

All About Smoothies!

SMOOTHIE MAKING BASICS

RECIPE AND ACTIVITY PAGES

MATH & MEASUREMENTS

SKILL BUILDING ACTIVITIES

FOOD SAFETY

GEOGRAPHY

SUBSTITUTIONS

FOOD ALLERGIES

FOOD SCIENCE

HEALTH

NUTRITION

CULINARY ARTS

CREATIVE WRITING ACTIVITIES

Other Resources Needed:

Be ready to use the internet, library books, an atlas, Google Earth or encyclopedias to research your smoothie making ingredients and cool places all over the world!

Use a #2 Pencil, smooth black pen, and colored pencils to complete the activities in this book.

FunSchoolingBooks.com

Do-It-Yourself

Get to know your fruits, veggies and more, on this nutrition focused, learning adventure!!

IT'S SMOOTHIE MAKING TIME

A Thinking Tree Production by:

Linda Janisse & Julia Stockman

Creative consultant: Heather Janisse

Cover: Tolik Trishkin   Producer: Sarah Janisse Brown

The Thinking
TREE

HOW TO USE THIS BOOK

In the next few pages we will describe the steps, basic instructions for food preparation, "prep", blending and safe food handling procedures.

These are basic recipes that use common ingredients to make prep easier. Some people have food allergies and different dietary needs. There is space after each one to rewrite it with any changes that you would like to make.

It is okay to experiment, use less or more of any ingredient. Try your own substitutions and flavor combinations. With every recipe, space is included, for you to journal and draw. There are more pages in the back of the book for notes, ideas, or overflow space to answer research questions! Use your imagination, be creative and have fun!!

MY CHECK LIST

Before you embark on your Smoothie Journey, here is a list of tools that you will need throughout the exploration and discovery:

- PARENT'S PERMISSION
- CLEAN HANDS OR GLOVES
- APRON (OPTIONAL)
- SMILING FACE
- BLENDER & LID
- MEASURING CUPS
- MEASURING SPOONS
- INGREDIENTS
- DRINKING CUPS
- DRINKING STRAWS

INSTRUCTIONS

VERY IMPORTANT:

Read and follow all safety and operating instructions that came with your blending device.

WITH ADULT PERMISSION:

1. Place and pour all ingredients in blender.
2. Secure lid on blender. (*If you have a cup/bullet style blender, follow the manufacturer's instructions.)
3. With a traditional blender, start blending on Low, slowly increase speed to High.
4. Blend until Smooth and Creamy.
5. Turn off the blender.
6. Pour and serve.
7. Add a straw/garnish. (optional)
8. Enjoy!
9. Remember to clean up.

FOOD SAFETY

◊ Wash your hands.

◊ Keep produce separated from any raw meat, poultry, seafood or eggs.

◊ To prevent dripping, NEVER store raw meat or poultry above produce in the fridge.

◊ Refrigerate perishable, cut or peeled produce.

◊ Remove damaged or bruised areas and discard rotten fruits and veggies.

◊ Wash thoroughly with water before eating, cutting or cooking.

◊ Scrub firm produce with a brush, under water.

◊ Make sure to always use a clean towel to dry produce. Or let it air dry.

TIP:

Use a separate cutting board for produce and meat products.

If you only have one, you can designate a side for each.

Always make sure that any prep area is properly cleaned

and sanitized before cutting produce.

WHAT IS CROSS-CONTAMINATION?

_____

_____

_____

_____

WHY IS IT IMPORTANT TO FOLLOW SAFE FOOD HANDLING PROCEDURES?

_____

_____

_____

LIST SOME FOOD-BORNE ILLNESSES, THAT CAN BE PREVENTED, BY PROPER FOOD HANDLING PROCEDURES.

_____

_____

_____

PRODUCE PREPARATION (PREP)

◊ Wash your hands/use gloves.

◊ Wash and dry fruits and veggies.

◊ Look up the best way to peel/cut/prep your smoothie making ingredients.

◊ Ask an adult for help with cutting/using a knife.

◊ Slice or chop fruits/veggies to use in smoothies. You can store them in the fridge to use within a few days.

◊ Don't forget to label and date anything that you won't be using immediately.

FREEZER PREP

◊ Lay prepped produce on a cookie sheet and freeze.

◊ Pour liquids into ice-cube trays and freeze, it takes about 3 hours.

◊ Once frozen, store prepped produce/liquid of choice (LOC) in freezer bags. Make sure that you label and date everything.

MIXED BERRY PREP

Place your choice of berries on a cookie sheet and freeze, label and bag together. In this book we made a mixture of equal parts: raspberry, blackberry, blueberry and cherry. You can also buy bags of frozen mixed berries in the freezer section of your local market.

COMMON KITCHEN TERMS

CAYG: **Clean As You Go!** Keep a tidy work space.

LDR: **Label, Date, Rotate!** Know how long you have had your food and what it is. For storage, place new food behind/under old.

FIFO: **First In, First Out!** Always use oldest food first, to avoid wasting precious food!

LIQUID OF CHOICE (LOC)

People have different dietary needs, texture, and flavor preferences. You are invited to be creative with your smoothie making.

Be encouraged to experiment with several liquids of choice.

Freeze your L.O.C. into cubes for a more "chill" smoothie!!

HERE IS AN LOC STARTER LIST.
SEE WHAT YOU CAN ADD TO IT.

ORANGE JUICE (OJ) _____

PINEAPPLE JUICE _____

CRANBERRY JUICE _____

APPLE JUICE _____

MILK _____

CHOCOLATE MILK _____

ORGANIC SOY MILK _____

ORGANIC RICE MILK _____

ALMOND MILK _____

COCONUT MILK _____

COCONUT WATER _____

GREEN TEA _____

KOMBUCHA _____

KEFIR _____

CLUB SODA _____

SMOOTHIE BOOSTERS!!

Have you heard about SUPER-FOODS? These are ingredients that can be added to your smoothie to increase nutritional value!

*Peanut Butter*Smoothie Booster*Peanut Butter*Power*

Here is a starter list, please be creative and see if you can find more items to add to it! Have Fun!

WHEAT GRASS _____

VITAMIN C POWDER _____

PROTEIN POWDER _____

CHIA SEEDS _____

FLAX SEED _____

PROBIOTIC POWDER _____

ALMOND BUTTER _____

CASHEW BUTTER _____

PEANUT BUTTER _____

YOGURT _____

PROTEIN POWDER _____

COCONUT OIL _____

MORINGA _____

TURMERIC POWDER _____

TIME TO MEASURE

There are quite a few ways to measure your ingredients. We picked the most common in the USA, which is Cups (C), Tablespoons (T), and Teaspoons (tsp.). Some people use ounces (oz.), in some places they use milliliters (mL). Another unit of measurement is grams (g). If you have a scale, you might like to try converting a recipe into grams. Pick whatever method you want to use, or try them all.

Conversions

1/4 cup	2 oz.	60 mL
1/2 cup	4 oz.	120 mL
3/4 cup	6 oz.	180 mL
1 cup	8 oz.	240 mL

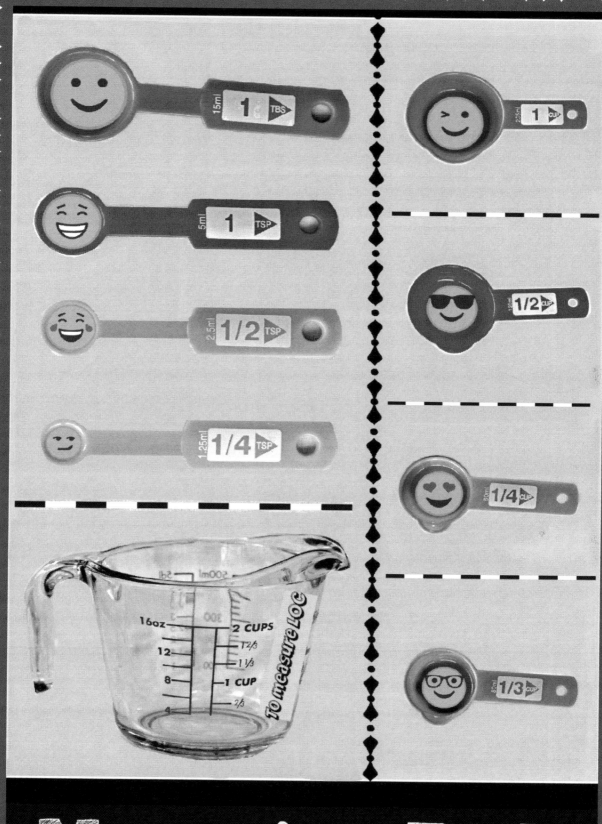

Measuring Tools

TOOLS

Blender

bullet/cup style blender

Scraper Spatulas

Always read and

Follow the

Instructions that

Come with your

Blending device.

CHEF'S KNIFE

Be very careful when using sharp tools. Have and adult help you to use them safely and properly.

SERRATED KNIFE

Safety First

PARING KNIFE

Ask for help.

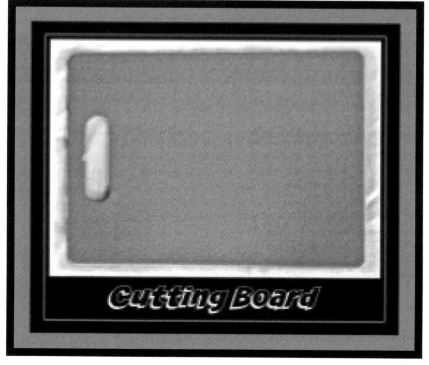

Cutting Board

Only cut your

produce on a

clean surface.

Adjective Garden

Frosty Creamy SMOOTH

Liquidy Silky

Bitter Vibrant

CHUNKY Yummy

SOUR THICK

Frothy

Zesty Sweet

Throughout this book, you will be asked to describe your smoothie creations. Use this space to write more adjectives. Be creative, try writing, the words you choose, in new ways using different fonts.

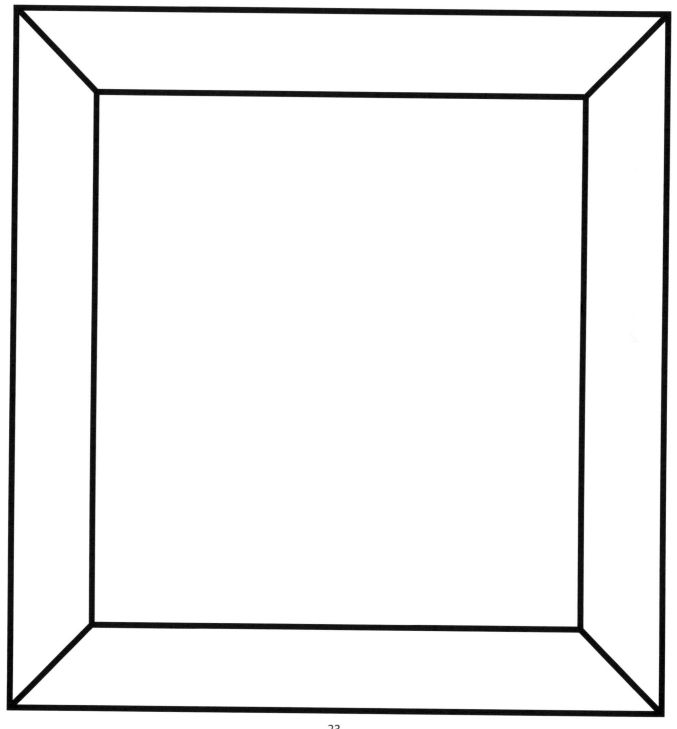

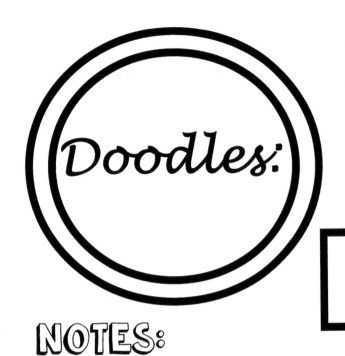

Doodles:

Make your own discovery pages for ingredients!

IDEAS:

NOTES:

Use these pages as your own creative space.

ART Space!

Ingredient List:

_____
_____
_____
_____
_____
_____
_____
_____
_____
_____
_____
_____

— ◊◈◊ —

Tip:

Always peel your bananas BEFORE freezing them!

Prep Steps:

_____
_____
_____
_____
_____
_____
_____

STRAWBERRY BANANA SMOOTHIE

1 frozen banana

5 or 6 frozen strawberries

1 Cup yogurt

½ Cup water or *LOC (*liquid of choice)

Re-write the recipe with your changes.

Q&A:

How did you like this smoothie?

_____

_____

_____

Describe the flavor, consistency, color and texture?

_____

_____

_____

Would you change anything next time?

_____

_____

_____

What *LOC did you use?

_____

_____

_____

What are some uses for banana peels?

_____

_____

_____

SCRUMPTIOUS STRAWBERRY

People love strawberries, in Florida, USA, they even have a strawberry festival!

What is your favorite way to prepare strawberries?

_____

_____

_____

_____

How and where are strawberries grown, what climate do they like?

_____

_____

_____

_____

What kind of fruit is a strawberry?

_____

_____

_____

_____

DRAW STRAWBERRIES GROWING.

What are the nutrition facts and health benefits of consuming strawberries?

_____

_____

_____

_____

Find a strawberry recipe and write it out. (If you need more room, write the title here and use a note page to write out your strawberry recipe.)

_____

_____

_____

_____

GO BANANAS!

THERE ARE MANY KINDS OF BANANAS. THEY GROW IN VARIOUS PLACES.

List some different kinds of bananas and where they are grown.

_____

_____

_____

_____

Ripe bananas are ready to peel and eat as they are. What are some other ways to use and/or prepare bananas?

_____

_____

_____

_____

How can you tell when a banana is ripe?

_____

_____

_____

_____

DRAW BANANAS GROWING.

What are some nutrition facts about bananas?

_____

_____

_____

_____

Bananas turn brown when they are cut and exposed to air. Why does this happen? How do you keep cut bananas fresh?

_____

_____

_____

_____

WORD SEARCH

```
Q G D T I U R F N O G A R D A
Y R R E B N A R C B E N T A G
Z A J Y Q C O W Y W Y T O K E
M P P S R P E H R I V H R J G
B E O G Y R R E B P S A R J N
E E Y S I F E A L R D U A V A
Y S E R E E V B H A N L C L R
T D E T R O C C K O K Y R M O
G R S L C E A K G C H Q V Z Y
C L C A P N B L C W A K Z L O
N G D V I P Y E K H D L Q Q O
W O G P Q T A D U W E I B H C
J Q S S X H A L T L K R J Q V
Y O N T C F A B J P B Q R L G
S I L W O E D Z O G N A M Y D
```

Cranberry	Cherry	Apples
Grape	Raspberry	Carrot
Orange	Blackberry	Beet
Spinach	Blueberry	Mango
Kale	Dragon Fruit	Avocado

Q: What do you call shoes made out of banana peel?

A: Slippers!

NOTES:

Farmers Market Special

Ingredient List:

_____
_____
_____
_____
_____
_____
_____
_____
_____
_____
_____

◇◈◇

Tip:

It is good to taste your smoothie, before you pour it. You can adjust the flavor, thickness or temperature. Sometimes a little more liquid, Ice, or honey, will make a big difference.

Prep Steps:

_____
_____
_____
_____
_____
_____

FARMER'S MARKET SPECIAL

3-5 cubes frozen cranberry juice

5 or 6 frozen strawberries

1/2 frozen banana

1 small handful of spinach leaves

1/3 cup yogurt

3/4 cup water or LOC

Re-write the recipe with your changes.

Q&A:

How did you like your finished product?

_____

_____

_____

Describe flavor, consistency, color and texture:

_____

_____

_____

What would you do differently?

_____

_____

_____

What LOC did you use?

_____

_____

_____

What did you learn?

_____

_____

_____

SUPER-DUPER SPINACH!

Spinach is a known as a "super food", packed with green goodness.

How and where is it grown? Can you grow spinach in your climate? How and where would you grow it?

_____

_____

_____

_____

How and when is spinach harvested?

_____

_____

_____

_____

List at least 5 different ways to prepare it, raw and/or cooked.

_____

_____

_____

_____

DRAW SPINACH GROWING.

List the nutrition facts and some health benefits of consuming spinach.

_____

_____

_____

_____

Find and write out a recipe that uses spinach as an ingredient.

_____

_____

_____

_____

Team Super-Duper Spinach

Caption this ...

NOTES:

_____

_____

_____

_____

_____

_____

_____

Ingredient List:

_____
_____
_____
_____
_____
_____
_____
_____
_____
_____

—— ◇◈◇ ——

Tip:
You can freeze leftover smoothie, from this Recipe, into amazing popsicles for a cool treat!

Prep Steps:

_____
_____
_____
_____
_____
_____
_____

THE SPECTACULAR ORANGE DREAMSICLE

½ cup orange juice (frozen into cubes)

½ cup vanilla almond milk

¼ cup orange juice* OJ*

1 tsp honey

Re-write the recipe with your changes.

Q&A:

How did you like this concoction?

_____

_____

_____

Describe flavor, consistency, color and texture:

_____

_____

_____

How would you improve this recipe?

_____

_____

_____

What could you substitute for almond milk to avoid nuts?

_____

_____

_____

How would you make this recipe creamier?

_____

_____

_____

HONEY IS YUMMY!

Honey can be used in place of other sweeteners.

What is honey? How is it made? What else do bees make?

_____

_____

_____

_____

Why are bees important to the survival of the human race?

_____

_____

_____

_____

What is the difference between raw and pasteurized honey?

_____

_____

_____

_____

DRAW A BEE COLLECTING POLLEN.

Many people like to consume raw, local honey. Why? List some nutrition facts and health benefits of honey.

_____

_____

_____

_____

Find a conversion ratio to substitute honey for sugar in recipes.

_____

_____

_____

_____

OUTSTANDING ORANGE!

Oranges are a very fun fruit, they can be peeled and eaten, right off the tree.

Oranges are grown all over the world, where do they originate from? How did they get to the Americas?

_____

_____

_____

_____

There are many varieties of oranges, list as many as you can.

_____

_____

_____

_____

Where are oranges grown, what is the climate like? What time of year are they harvested? How are they harvested?

_____

_____

_____

_____

DRAW ORANGES GROWING.

Look up nutrition information about oranges and list a few facts.

_____

_____

_____

_____

Most everyone likes orange Juice, or OJ, for short. List other ways to use the orange. What can you do with the peel?

_____

_____

_____

_____

Mr. Orange

NOTES:

_____

_____

_____

_____

_____

_____

_____

_____

_____

_____

Sweet Sea Foamy Delight

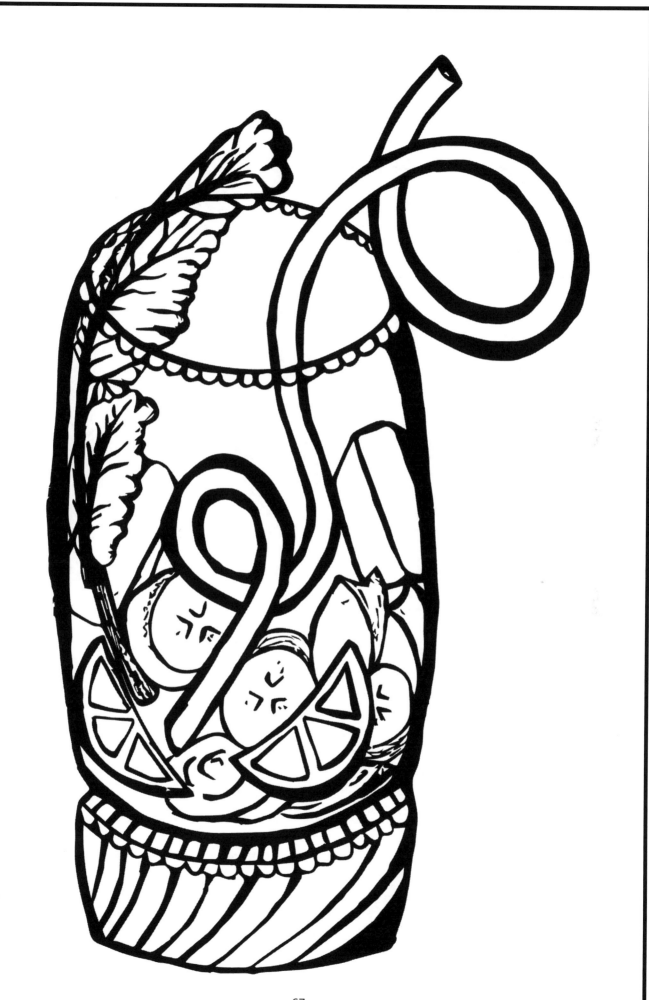

Ingredient List:

_____
_____
_____
_____
_____
_____
_____
_____
_____
_____
_____
_____

——— ◇·◇·◇ ———

Tip:

Use plain Yogurt to cut back on sugar and/ or sweetness.

Prep Steps:

_____
_____
_____
_____
_____
_____
_____

SWEET SEA FOAMY DELIGHT

4 cubes of frozen cranberry juice

1 large banana (peeled & frozen)

1 small handful of kale

1 thin slice of ginger

¼ lemon

1 cup yogurt

1 cup water or LOC

1 T honey (optional)

Re-write the recipe with your changes.

Q&A:

How did you like this Smoothie?

_____

_____

_____

Describe flavor, consistency, color and texture:

_____

_____

_____

What would you do differently if you made it again?

_____

_____

_____

What LOC did you use?

_____

_____

_____

How would you make it more/less spicy?

_____

_____

_____

KALE IS COOL!!

Kale is a superfood and can be prepared many ways.

There are many varieties of Kale, please list and describe some.

_____

_____

_____

_____

How and where is Kale grown?

_____

_____

_____

_____

There are many ways to prepare kale. List some below.

_____

_____

_____

_____

DRAW KALE GROWING.

Write the nutrition facts about kale.

_____

_____

_____

_____

Kale goes nicely in green smoothies. Find a recipe to try and write it below. Did you like it?

_____

_____

_____

_____

HELLO GINGER!

Ginger has been the
spice of choice
for this smoothie book.
It is packed full
of goodness.

What is ginger? How does it grow?

_____

_____

_____

_____

**Where is it most commonly found/grown? What climate does it
live in?**

_____

_____

_____

_____

**Besides adding it to your smoothies raw, how else can it be pre-
pared?**

_____

_____

_____

_____

DRAW GINGER GROWING.

Find a recipe with ginger as an ingredient and write it out.

_____

_____

_____

_____

What is the nutritional value and health benefits of consuming ginger? List some facts.

_____

_____

_____

_____

HAVE YOUR KALE AND EAT IT TOO!

NOTES:

_____

_____

_____

_____

_____

_____

_____

_____

_____

Cherry Pucker

Ingredient List:

Tip:

You can squeeze your own lemons and zest them, then freeze into cubes. One cube can replace ¼ lemon.

Prep Steps:

CHERRY PUCKER

3 cubes frozen cranberry juice

12 cherries (pitted and frozen)

1/4 Cup of OJ

1/4 lemon

1/2 cup water or *LOC

Re-write the recipe with your changes.

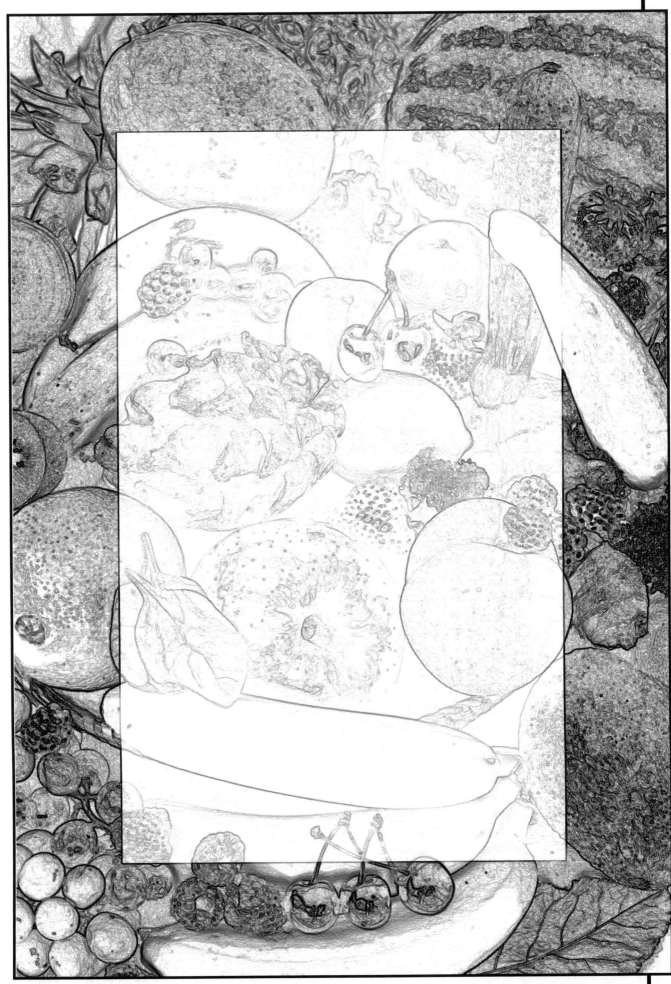

Q&A:

How did you like this Smoothie?

_____

_____

_____

Describe flavor, consistency, color and texture.

_____

_____

_____

How would you improve this recipe?

_____

_____

_____

What *LOC did you use, how well did it work?

_____

_____

_____

What variety of Cherry did you use?

_____

_____

_____

LOVELY LEMON!

Lemons are another very popular fruit of the citrus family!

You can add a slice of lemon to drinking water to improve the flavor and make it more alkaline.

How and where are lemons grown?

_____

_____

_____

_____

Name some varieties of lemon. What kind is most commonly found where you live?

_____

_____

_____

_____

Lemons aren't just for food. They have many uses. What are some ways lemons can be used around the house?

_____

_____

_____

_____

DRAW LEMONS GROWING.

List the nutrition facts and some health benefits of the lemon.

_____

_____

_____

_____

Lemon oil is a wonderful product. List some different uses for it.

_____

_____

_____

_____

CHERRY CHEER!

Cherries too, come in two different types, and many different varieties. What are the two types? List some of the varieties.

_____

_____

_____

_____

How and where do cherries grow?

_____

_____

_____

_____

Cherries like many other fruit, can be prepared in many ways. List five or more ways to use/prepare/serve cherries.

_____

_____

_____

_____

DRAW CHERRIES GROWING:

List the nutrition information on the cherry. How are cherries related to roses?

_____

_____

_____

_____

There are several ways to remove cherry pits. How do factories pit cherries? What is the easiest home method to pit a cherry?

_____

_____

_____

_____

WORD SEARCH

```
                    Q B U
              I S H M Z P I L V
            S W K K S K T U D Y N Q T
          P C O K L I M E T A L O C O H C O
        T P V V I C I O H X S C R O S B A B S
      L C H O M P L W S K J J R E H K D R N J K
      K U K T I K U N H O N B D H P X T J T X V
    O A S U M V       D C K B E       T H E P H B
    U S N E V N       X R Q N F       D J D I C C
  S K O R G W H E A T G R A S S W P M M N A I Y I M
  J C F N L I K E H H O R G A N I C S O Y M I L K S
  O V T W J X F G A W K H A K H C L T E H S P X A J
  C J D R E D W O P N I E T O R P N M P M Q K I T E C B
  Q O R G A N I C R I C E M I L K I O U H H E W Y T M I
  U A S C H I A S E E D S U K B S C O L O M E Z X N R X
  U L K C   Z Y Q I G V P M W D L I H U I     O E E R
  F Q M Q     T I S Z M K N R I F E K I       X N E U
  G A J O H     T S J A P U B P K Q O       D T Q R H
  L H S N L                           R H I L G
  O V C C D S                         E C S R B Z
      V K U L M C R D G Q N C W V V K S E A H E
      M C R B U I E T U R M E R I C P O W D E R
        W Y O M B L F Y I K L A V Y G C R A G
        H Z Q O S K G J S H B B M D R R J
          E O K O Y O S W X J J H Y
            W J D U F J R D U
                A Z C
```

CLUB SODA

WHEAT GRASS

PROTEIN POWDER

MILK

GREEN TEA

CHOCOLATE MILK

TURMERIC POWDER

ORGANIC SOY MILK

PROTEIN POWDER

COCONUT WATER

ORGANIC RICE MILK

KOMBUCHA

COCONUT MILK

KEFIR

CHIA SEEDS

NOTES:

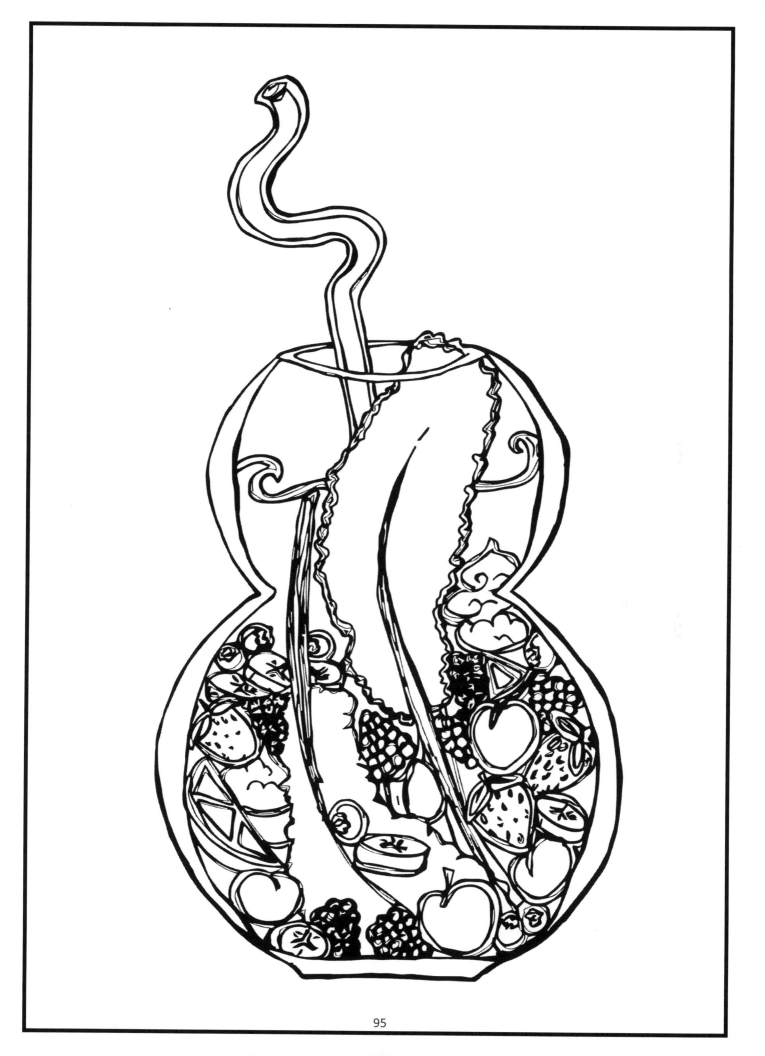

Q&A:

How did you like the Very Berry Fruit Smoothie?

_____

_____

_____

Describe flavor, consistency, color and texture:

_____

_____

_____

How would you improve this recipe?

_____

_____

_____

What L.O.C. did you use? How was the result?

_____

_____

_____

*This recipe used equal parts frozen raspberry, blackberry, blueberry and cherry.

What does your frozen berry mix consist of?

_____

_____

_____

Ingredient List:

_____
_____
_____
_____
_____
_____
_____
_____
_____
_____
_____

—————— ◇◈◇ ——————

Tip:

Kale stalks are very fibrous. For smoothie making, it is best to strip the leaves from the stalk. The leftover stalks can be frozen, and kept with other vege-table scraps, to boil later and make homemade veggie stock.

Prep Steps:

_____
_____
_____
_____
_____
_____

VERY BERRY FRUIT SMOOTHIE

½ cup frozen *mixed berries

2-3 strawberries (fresh or frozen)

½ banana (peeled & frozen)

1 small handful of kale

1 thin slice of ginger

¼ lemon squeezed

½ cup yogurt

1 cup OJ

¼ cup water or LOC

Re-write the recipe with your changes.

RASPBERRY*raspeberry*RASPBERRY*raspberry

MERRY RASPBERRY!

The Raspberries that we usually find in the grocery store are usually bright red. Did you know that they come in many different varieties and colors? List some different types and colors below:

_____

_____

_____

_____

Describe where and how raspberries grow.

_____

_____

_____

_____

Raspberries are delicious to just pick and eat! There are also many other ways to prepare them. List some ways that raspberries are commonly prepared/eaten.

_____

_____

_____

_____

DRAW RASPBERRIES GROWING.

List the nutrition facts about Raspberries:

_____

_____

_____

_____

In looking up nutrition facts in this journal, you have probably come across the term "anti-oxidant". Please define what an anti-oxidant is and why that should matter to a person.

_____

_____

_____

_____

BEAUTIFUL BLACKBERRY!

Blackberries grow two ways, erect canes and trailing vines. How and where do they grow?

_____

_____

_____

_____

There are many names and varieties of blackberries, list some.

_____

_____

_____

_____

Like most berries, they are fun to pick and eat. There are also many great recipes that use them as an ingredient. List five or more ways to prepare/preserve blackberries.

_____

_____

_____

_____

DRAW BLACKBERRIES GROWING.

List the nutrition facts about blackberries:

_____

_____

_____

_____

What is a polyphenol? What is Manganese? How does it help brain function?

_____

_____

_____

_____

Berry Interesting:

1. Write the definition of a berry below.
2. Color the berries in this collage.

Ingredient List:

_____
_____
_____
_____
_____
_____
_____
_____
_____
_____
_____
_____

—◇◇◇—

Tip:

You can use your avocado seed to grow a new plant.

Prep Steps:

_____
_____
_____
_____
_____
_____
_____

FRUITY BLAST SMOOTHIE

3-5 frozen strawberries

15-20 frozen blueberries

5-7 frozen grapes

½ frozen banana

½ avocado (peeled and seeded)

¼ lemon

½ cup almond milk

Re-write the recipe with your changes.

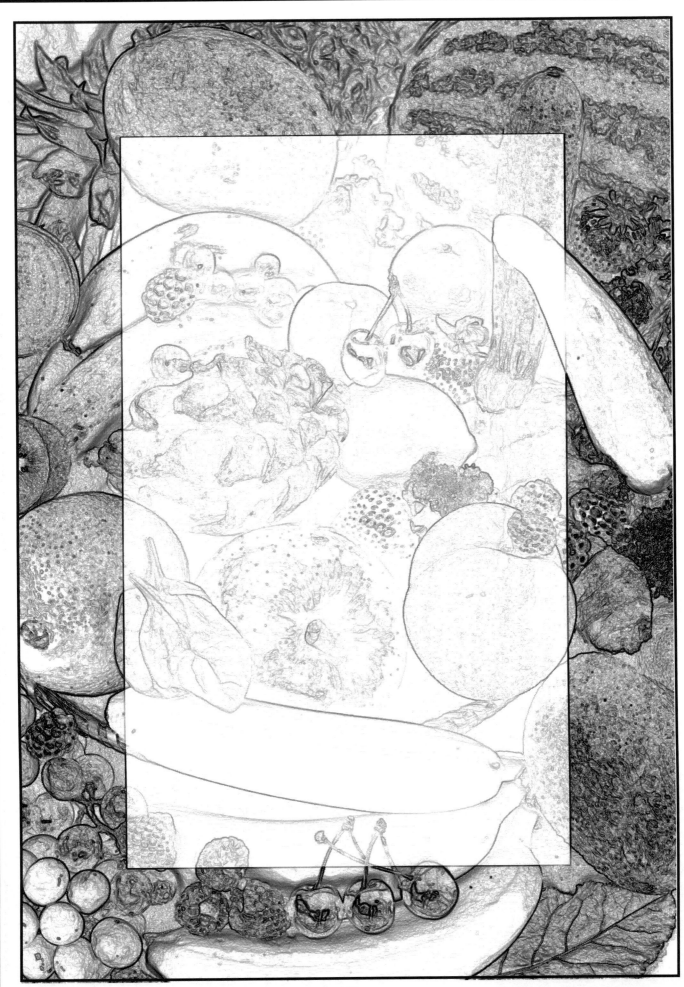

Q&A:

How did you like the Fruity Blast Smoothie?

_____

_____

_____

Describe flavor, consistency, color and texture.

_____

_____

_____

How would you improve this recipe?

_____

_____

_____

Why do you think that the word "Blast" is in the title?

_____

_____

_____

How do people prepare avocado seeds for consumption?

_____

_____

_____

VERY BLUEBERRY!

Many people have fond memories of going blueberry picking as children. They grow all over the United States of America and around the world.

Describe how and where blueberries grow.

_____

_____

_____

_____

Blueberries are great to eat as they are, but are also great when added to recipes. Name five or more ways to prepare/preserve blueberries.

_____

_____

_____

_____

If you were to go blueberry picking, where would you need to travel to? How would you get there?

_____

_____

_____

_____

DRAW BLUEBERRIES GROWING.

List some nutrition facts about blueberries.

_____

_____

_____

_____

What is your favorite way to enjoy blueberries?

_____

_____

_____

_____

GRAPE GOODNESS!

There are so many varieties of grapes, list a few different kinds.

_____

_____

_____

_____

Grapes grow all over the world. List some countries where grapes are grown.

_____

_____

_____

_____

How do grapes grow? What kind of climate do they flourish in?

_____

_____

_____

_____

DRAW GRAPES GROWING:

Look up the nutrition facts about grapes and list them below.

_____

_____

_____

_____

Grapes taste great straight off the vine. They are good for juice as well. What are other ways that grapes can be enjoyed?

_____

_____

_____

_____

NOTES:

_____

_____

_____

_____

_____

_____

_____

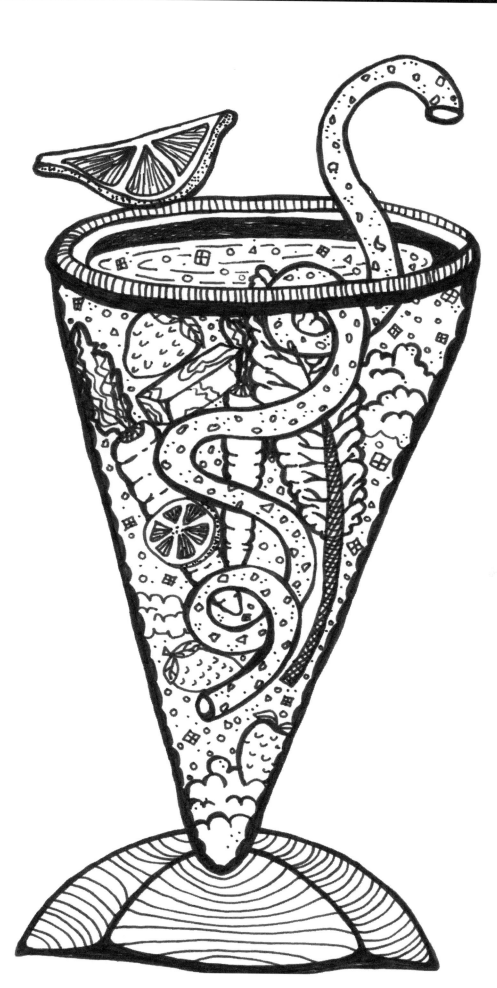

Ingredient List:

_____
_____
_____
_____
_____
_____
_____
_____
_____
_____
_____

— ◇◈◇ —

Tip:
Ginger can be prepared and frozen for quick smoothie prep and to preserve freshness.

Prep Steps:

_____
_____
_____
_____
_____
_____
_____

CREAMY SPICE & GINGER IS NICE

3 cubes frozen cranberry juice

3-5 frozen strawberries

1 small handful of kale

1 Carrot

1 thin slice of ginger

¼ lemon squeezed (or 1 cube)

1 cup vanilla yogurt

1 cup ginger ale

Re-write the recipe with your changes.

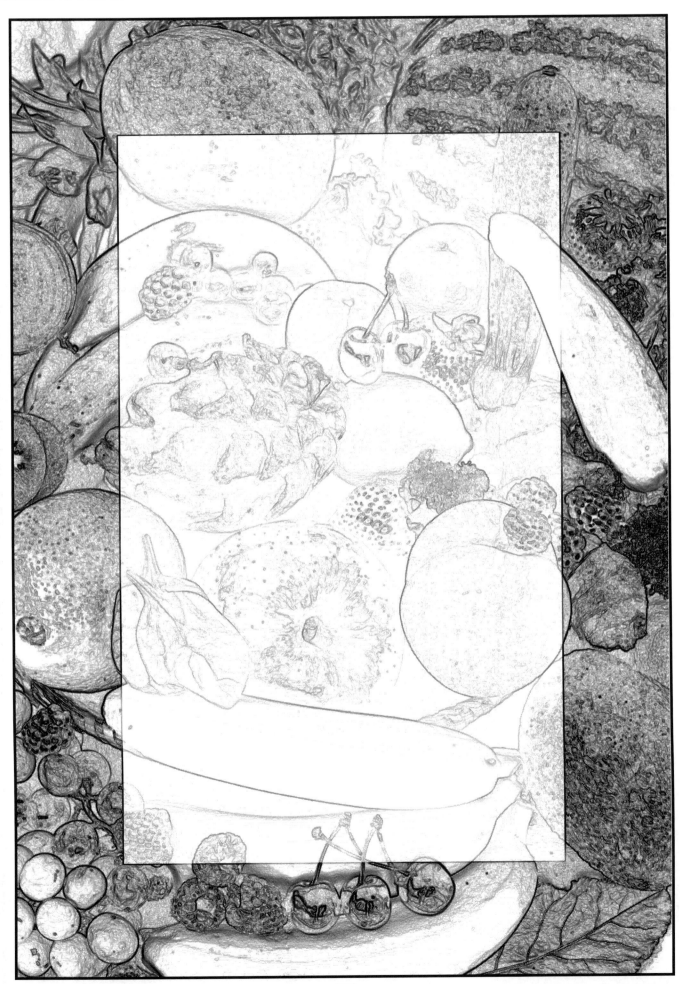

Q&A:

How did you like this smoothie?

_____

_____

_____

Describe flavor, consistency, color and texture.

_____

_____

_____

What adjustments might you make for next time?

_____

_____

_____

What other *LOC could you use to give it fizz?

_____

_____

_____

What could you substitute for yogurt to make this recipe vegan?

_____

_____

_____

YO YOGURT!

Yogurt is another superfood. People all over the world make it in one form or another. It is a great probiotic, and a great way to make a smoothie more creamy.

What exactly is yogurt and how is it made?

_____

_____

_____

_____

What are some of the health benefits of consuming yogurt?

_____

_____

_____

_____

What are some ways that yogurt is used around the world?

_____

_____

_____

_____

DRAW FRUITS THAT CAN FLAVOR YOGURT

List the nutrition facts about yogurt.

_____

_____

_____

_____

What are probiotics and what health benefits they provide?

_____

_____

_____

_____

Ginger

HELLO GINGER!

Ginger is a main flavor choice in this smoothie book. It is packed full of spicy goodness, and is used in many different ways.

What is ginger? How does it grow?

_____

_____

_____

_____

Where is ginger commonly grown?

_____

_____

_____

_____

Besides adding it to your smoothies raw, how else can it be prepared?

_____

_____

_____

_____

DRAW A PICTURE OF GINGER GROWING.

List the nutrition facts and health benefits of consuming ginger?

_____

_____

_____

_____

Find a recipe, with ginger as an ingredient, and write it out

_____

_____

_____

_____

FREE SPACE:

Ingredient List:

_____
_____
_____
_____
_____
_____
_____
_____
_____
_____
_____

◇ ◈ ◇

Tip:
You can freeze your
leftover smoothie in ice
cube trays and bag to
use again in other
smoothies.

Prep Steps:

_____
_____
_____
_____
_____
_____
_____

CREAMY GREEN TEAM

3-5 frozen strawberries

1 frozen banana

4 OJ cubes

½ avocado

1 small handful of spinach

½ cup vanilla yogurt

1 cup almond milk

Re-write the recipe with your changes.

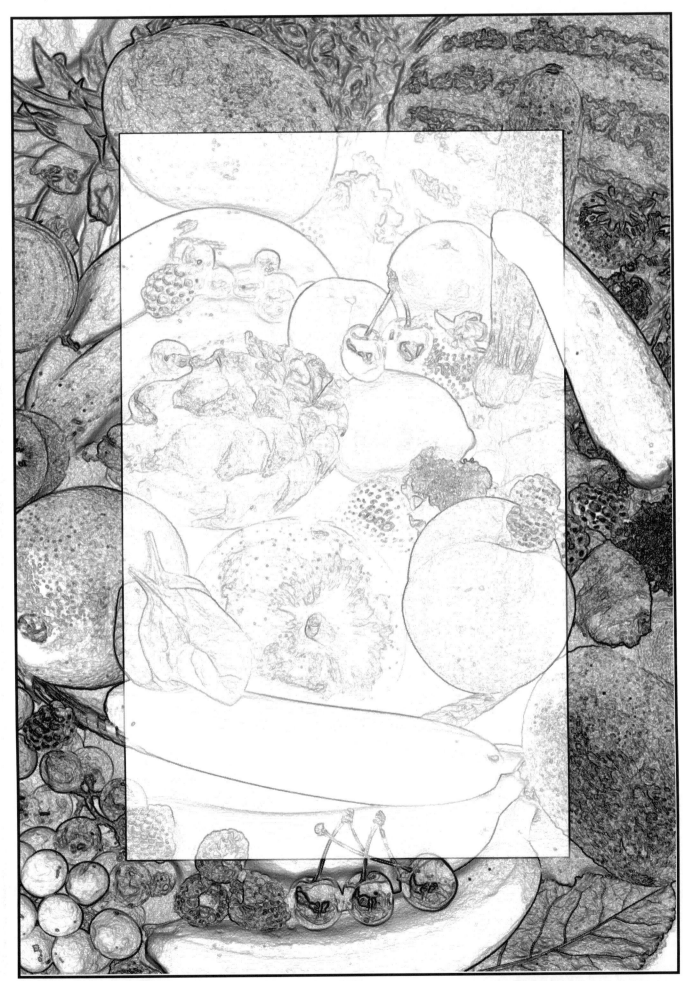

Q&A:

How did you like this Smoothie?

_____

_____

Describe flavor, consistency, color and texture:

_____

_____

_____

What would you do differently next time?

_____

_____

_____

What other "greens" could you substitute for spinach?

_____

_____

_____

How would you describe this smoothie to a friend?

_____

_____

_____

OH AVOCADO!

Avocado is very popular because it is packed with creamy goodness.

There are many different varieties, list at least five and where each is grown.

_____

_____

_____

_____

How do avocados grow? What kind of climate do they thrive in?

_____

_____

_____

_____

How do you select them at the market? How can you tell when an avocado is ripe? What is the best way to ripen them?

_____

_____

_____

_____

DRAW SOME AVOCADOS GROWING.

List the nutrition facts and health benefits of the avocado.

_____

_____

_____

_____

List a few different ways to prepare or serve avocado.

_____

_____

_____

_____

NOTES:

_____

_____

_____

_____

_____

_____

_____

_____

_____

Ingredient List:

_____

_____

_____

_____

_____

_____

_____

_____

_____

_____

_____

_____

———— ◇◈◇ ————

Tip:
You can make this more tangy and slightly effervescent by adding a tart kombucha as your liquid of choice.

Prep Steps:

_____

_____

_____

_____

_____

_____

_____

SUMMER SPLASH

4 frozen OJ cubes

3-6 frozen strawberries

1 frozen banana

¼ lemon

1 cup vanilla yogurt

1 cup water or LOC

Re-write the recipe with your changes.

❄

 Q&A:

How did you like this Smoothie?

_____

_____

_____

Describe flavor, consistency, color and texture:

_____

_____

_____

How would you change this recipe?

_____

_____

_____

What *LOC did you use? Why?

_____

_____

_____

Did it taste the way that you imagined it would?

_____

_____

_____

NOTES AND DOODLES:

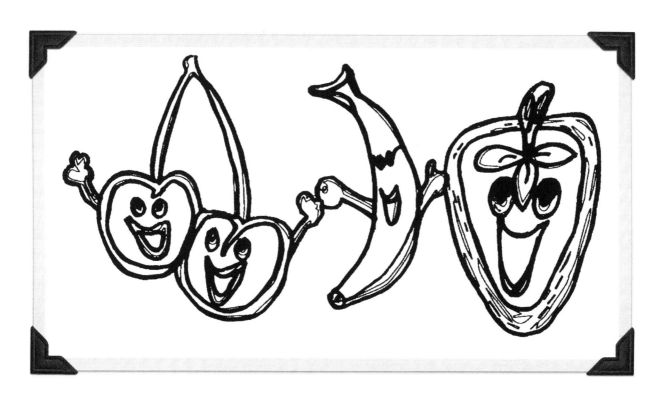

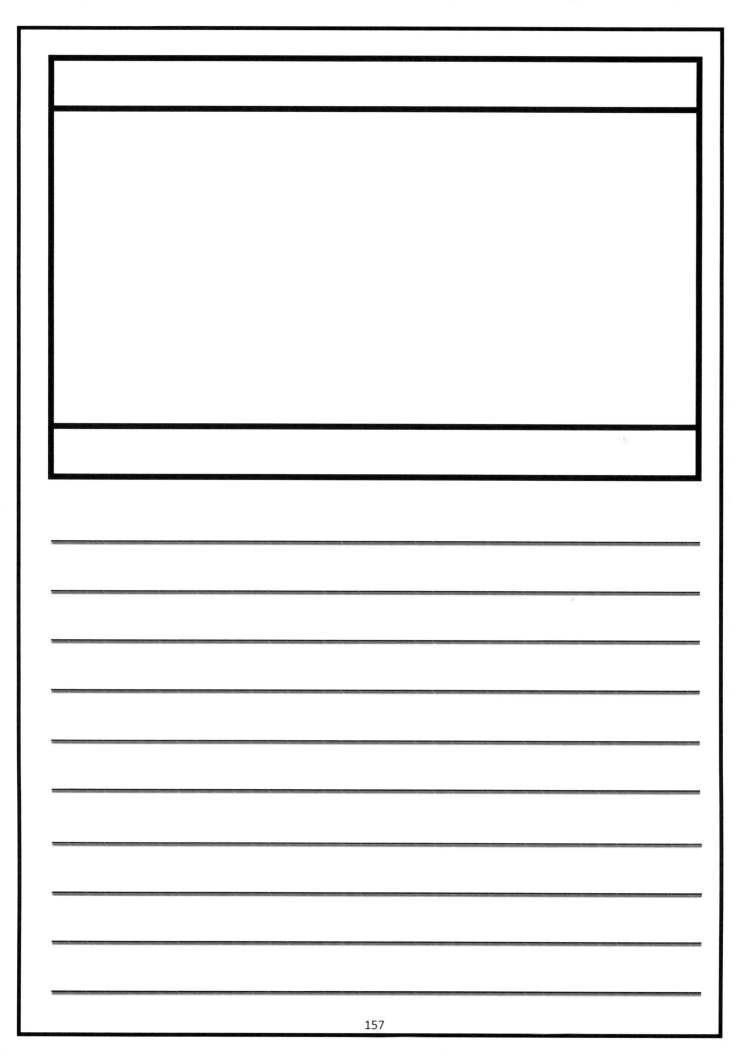

Ingredient List:

_____
_____
_____
_____
_____
_____
_____
_____
_____
_____
_____
_____

◇◈◇

Tip:
Veggies that are getting too ripe can be chopped & frozen, or smashed into ice cube trays to enjoy later in a smoothie!

Prep Steps:

_____
_____
_____
_____
_____
_____
_____

PRETTY PURPLE SMOOTHIE

4 frozen OJ cubes

1 frozen banana

12 pitted cherries (fresh or frozen)

½ of a dragon fruit or beet (or ¼ of each)

1 cup vanilla yogurt

1 cup pineapple juice

Re-write the recipe with your changes.

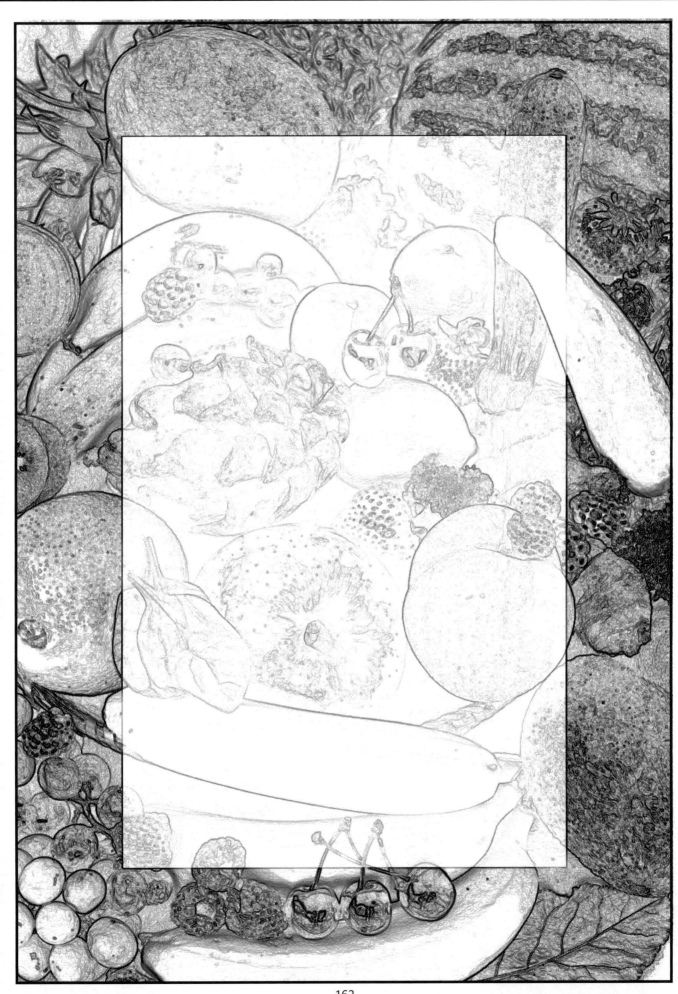

Q&A:

How did you like this Smoothie?

_____

_____

_____

Describe flavor, consistency, color and texture.

_____

_____

_____

How would you improve this recipe?

_____

_____

_____

Did you use Dragon Fruit, if yes, what color?

_____

_____

_____

Would you recommend this smoothie to a friend?

_____

_____

_____

WOW DRAGON FRUIT!!

Many people have never heard of it or tried it. It is a truly beautiful and unique fruit.

What kind of plant produces Dragon Fruit? Where does it grow? List the varieties?

_____

_____

_____

_____

How is dragon fruit commonly prepared/served? How do you tell if it is ripe?

_____

_____

_____

Describe the color and texture of the part of the fruit that people eat.

_____

_____

_____

DRAW A PICTURE OF DRAGON FRUIT GROWING.

List the nutrition facts and health benefits of consuming Dragon Fruit.

_____

_____

_____

_____

Where would you buy dragon fruit near you? Have you ever tried it? If yes, did you like it?

_____

_____

_____

WORD SEARCH

```
            P   Y
          Z   N   I   R
        Z   W   A   O   N   R
      Y   Q   S   L   E   M   E   E
    C   H   D   I   M   C   O   E   A   B
  R   B   N   R   M   O   I   C   V   L   P   W
L   N   Y   N   H   M   N   U   R   F   W   E   P   A
  G   T   U   E   A   C   Z   D   J   A   P   F   S   Y   L   R
U   R   N   J   G   P   X   D   B   E   N   J   Q   W   K   O   E   T
R   D   G   B   C   I   P   F   Y   U   L   B   J   C   U   C   L   V   N   S
P   A   L   M   E   N   L   L   V   T   P   E   Y   G   I   O   E   U   X   F
  J   J   F   B   G   E   A   N   T   P   R   T   R   U   G   O   Y   G
    B   T   O   E   J   X   W   E   A   R   Y   J   W   P   I   J
      N   L   R   U   S   M   R   E   Y   I   R   M   T   H
        G   L   I   E   A   J   N   J   S   C   N   O
          B   C   E   I   C   I   U   Z   J   N
            E   D   D   P   P   I   Z   E
              S   A   L   W   C   Y
                J   E   K   E
                  A   A
```

Flax Seeds	Strawberry	Lemon
Probiotic Powder	Orange Juice	Ginger
Almond Butter	Pineapple Juice	Honey
Cashew Butter	Cranberry Juice	Yogurt
Peanut Butter	Apple Juice	Pineapple

NOTES:

_____

_____

_____

_____

_____

_____

_____

_____

_____

_____

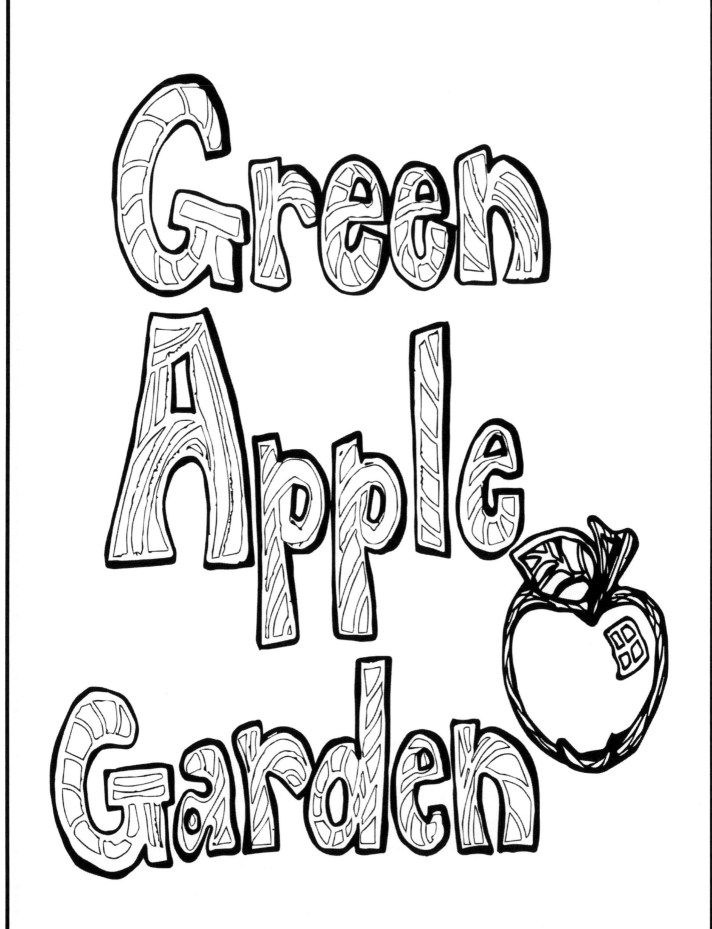

Ingredient List:

_____
_____
_____
_____
_____
_____
_____
_____
_____
_____

———————— ◇◇◇ ————————

Tip:
You can spread chopped greens out on a cookie sheet to freeze. Transfer into a storage bag, to use later.

Prep Steps:

_____
_____
_____
_____
_____

GREEN APPLE GARDEN

6 frozen OJ cubes

½ green apple

1 carrot

1 small handful of beet greens

2/3 cup vanilla yogurt

2/3 cup pineapple juice

1/2 cup orange juice

1 T honey

Re-write the recipe with your changes.

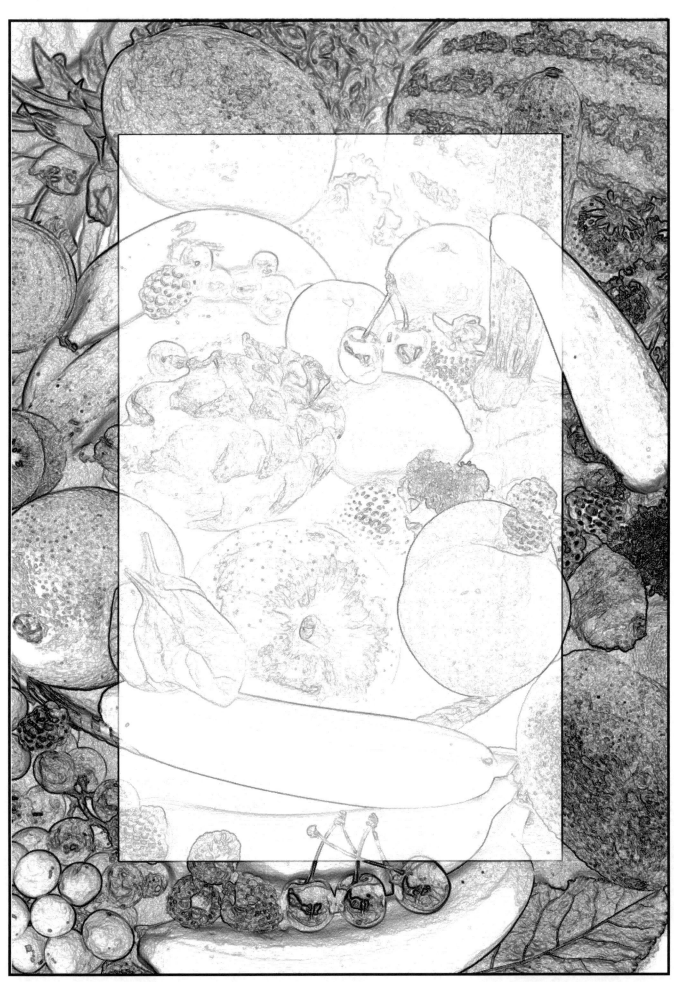

Q&A:

How did you like this recipe?

_____

_____

_____

Describe flavor, consistency, color and texture.

_____

_____

_____

How would you make it more nutritious?

_____

_____

_____

What other veggies could you add to this smoothie?

_____

_____

_____

What did you learn?

_____

_____

_____

Applause for Apples!

Apples come in many varieties and are grown in many places.

List five or more distinct types of apples, and where they are grown.

_____

_____

_____

_____

We can eat raw apples straight from the tree. What are other ways to use/prepare apples?

_____

_____

_____

_____

What is your favorite type of apple? How do you like to prepare them?

_____

_____

_____

_____

Draw a picture of an apple growing.

Look up the nutrition facts about the apple and list them below:

_____

_____

_____

_____

Apples get "rusty", when they are sliced and exposed to air. Why does this happen? How do you keep cut apples looking fresh?

_____

_____

_____

_____

Carrot me away!

Most carrots that we see in the market are orange, but they come in many other colors too!

List some kinds and colors of carrots and how and where they grow.

_____

_____

_____

_____

Carrots are great raw, but there are other ways to prepare them too. List five or more ways to prepare carrots.

_____

_____

_____

_____

If you were going to plant carrots in your garden, how would you proceed? What would you need?

_____

_____

_____

_____

Draw a picture of a carrot growing.

List the nutrition facts and the potential health benefits of ingesting carrots.

_____

_____

_____

_____

Write your favorite carrot recipe.

_____

_____

_____

_____

Ingredient List:

_____
_____
_____
_____
_____
_____
_____
_____
_____
_____
_____
_____
_____

—◇—◇—◇—

Tip:
Wear gloves & an apron, because beet juice will stain your hands & clothing.

Prep Steps:

_____
_____
_____
_____
_____
_____
_____

BERRY DELIGHTFUL

6 OJ cubes

½ cup frozen mixed berries

5-8 frozen red seedless grapes

2 slices of beet

1 small slice of ginger

1 Heaping T Greek vanilla yogurt

1 cup almond milk

2 T honey

Re-write the recipe with your changes.

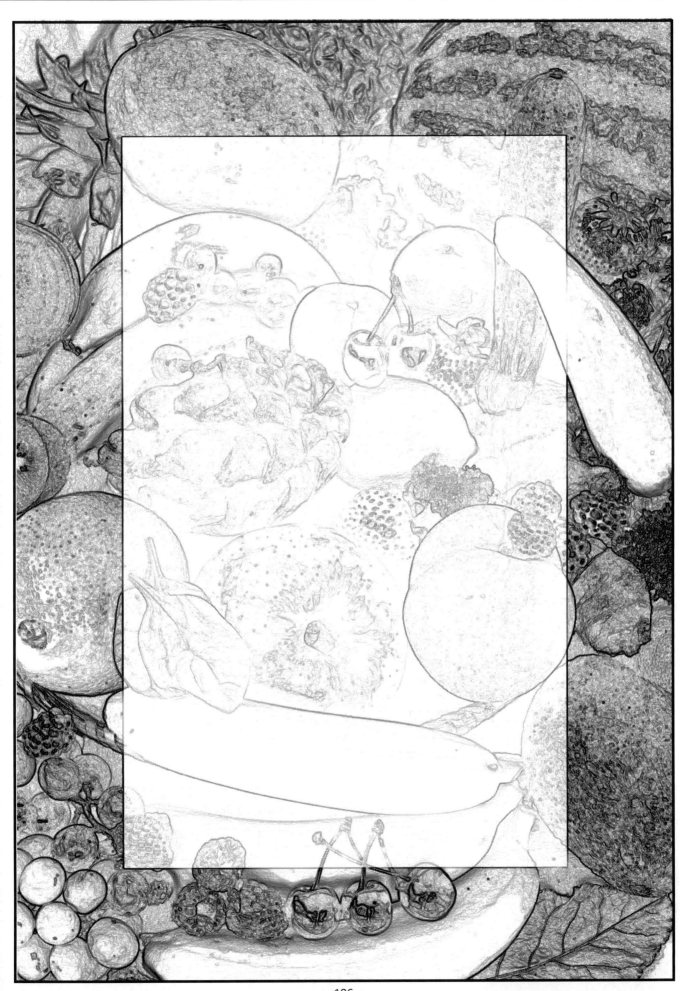

Q&A:

How did you like this Smoothie?

_____

_____

_____

Describe flavor, consistency, color and texture:

_____

_____

_____

What would you change for next time?

_____

_____

_____

How many cups did the smoothie yield?

_____

_____

_____

What could you use in place of frozen OJ Cubes?

_____

_____

_____

Sliced Beets ~ Drop the beet! ~ Pickled Beets ~ Can't be beet!

CAN'T BE BEET!

Beets are a root veggie and their greens are good to eat too!

Most people think of beets being dark red or purple, but they come in other colors too. List some varieties of beets and where they grow.

_____

_____

_____

_____

List some ways to use/prepare beets and beet-greens.

_____

_____

_____

_____

A favorite way to prepare beets in the USA is to pickle and can them. For many generations, people have canned their own food at home to preserve it. Describe the canning process.

_____

_____

_____

_____

DRAW A PICTURE OF A BEET GROWING.

Look up the nutrition information on beets and beet-greens, list it below.

_____

_____

_____

_____

Find a beet recipe and write it out below.

_____

_____

_____

_____

Milk

ALL ABOUT MILK!

Everyone knows that milk comes from cows, right? But for many reasons, people consume other "milks". Goat's milk for one. Milk is also made from different kinds of nuts.

List the steps that cow's milk goes through from farm to table?

_____

_____

_____

_____

Why do some people prefer "raw" milk? What is the perceived benefit?

_____

_____

_____

_____

Describe the process of making almond milk.

_____

_____

_____

_____

ILLUSTRATE YOUR FAVORITE MILK.

List the nutrition facts and health benefits of your favorite milk.

_____

_____

_____

_____

List some reasons why people might choose a non-dairy form of milk over cow's milk.

_____

_____

_____

_____

Ingredient List:

_____
_____
_____
_____
_____
_____
_____
_____
_____
_____
_____
_____

—◇•◇—

Tip:

You can combine frozen fruit and cubes into individual bags for quick smoothie prep. Just add your favorite LOC and blend. Yogurt can be frozen into cubes too! Remember to label and date!!

Prep Steps:

_____
_____
_____
_____
_____
_____
_____

TROPICAL MELT

4 pineapple juice cubes

½ frozen banana

5-7 strawberries

½ a mango

2 T Greek yogurt

¾ Cup coconut milk

1 T honey

Re-write the recipe with your changes.

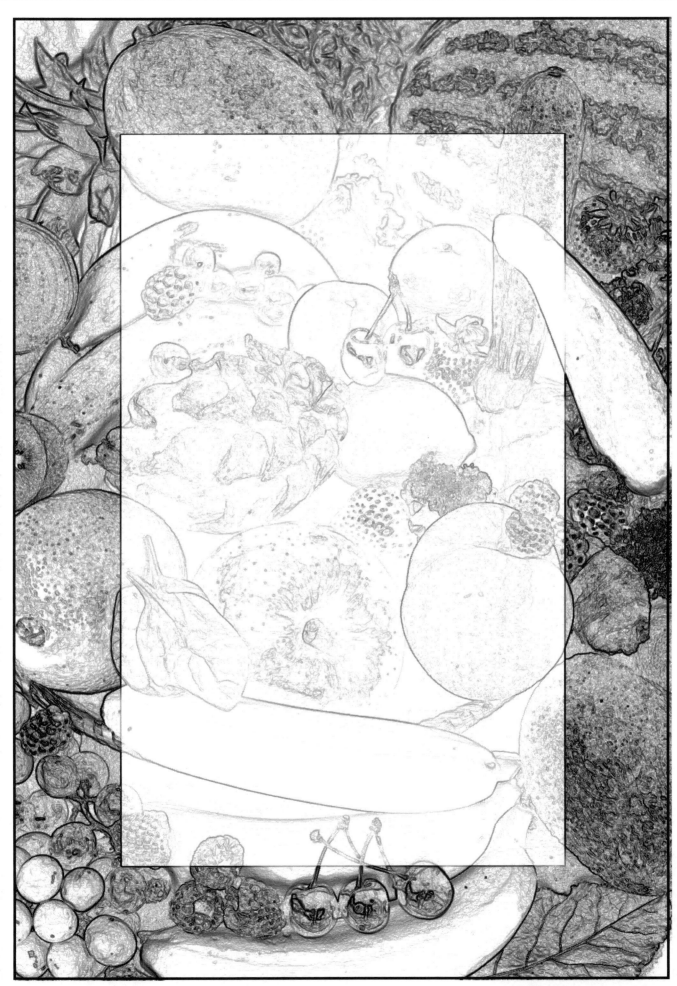

Q&A:

How did you like this Smoothie?

_____

_____

_____

Describe flavor, color and texture:

_____

_____

_____

How would you improve this recipe?

_____

_____

_____

What fruit could you substitute for strawberries?

_____

_____

_____

Do you have a friend that would like this smoothie?

_____

_____

_____

Aloha Pineapple!

Pineapple is a tropical fruit, and the juice is a favorite ingredient in drink recipes.

How and where is pineapple grown?

_____

_____

_____

_____

How can you grow a pineapple?

_____

_____

_____

_____

What is your favorite way to consume pineapple?

_____

_____

_____

_____

Draw a pineapple growing.

List the nutrition facts and health benefits of the pineapple.

_____

_____

_____

_____

Find and write out a pineapple recipe.

_____

_____

_____

_____

MARVELOUS MANGO!

Marvelous Mango

You shouldn't judge a book by its cover;

and you can't tell if a mango is ripe

by looking at its color.

Mangos are a favorite fruit all over the world. But do you know where they originally came from? Write a brief history of the mango.

_____

_____

_____

_____

Mangos come in many different types and are from many different places. List some different varieties and where they are grown.

_____

_____

_____

_____

How do you tell if a mango is ready to eat? How do you speed up the ripening process? How do you slow it?

_____

_____

_____

_____

DRAW A MANGO GROWING.

List the nutrition facts about mangos.

_____

_____

_____

_____

Mangos are great to peel and eat, just as they are, but you can use them in recipes too! List a few ways to use/prepare mangos.

_____

_____

_____

_____

Ingredient List:

_____
_____
_____
_____
_____
_____
_____
_____
_____
_____
_____

———◇◆◇———

Tip:

You can freeze any *LOC into cubes and then store in a freezer bag for later use. Make sure to label and date your items!

As a substitute for chocolate milk, you can use any other milk and add a Tbsp. of Black-Strap Molasses.

Prep Steps:

_____
_____
_____
_____
_____
_____
_____

CHOCOLATE BANANA NUT MILK-SHAKE

2 bananas (peeled & frozen)

2 Cups chocolate Milk

¼ Cup peanut butter

Re-write the recipe with your changes.

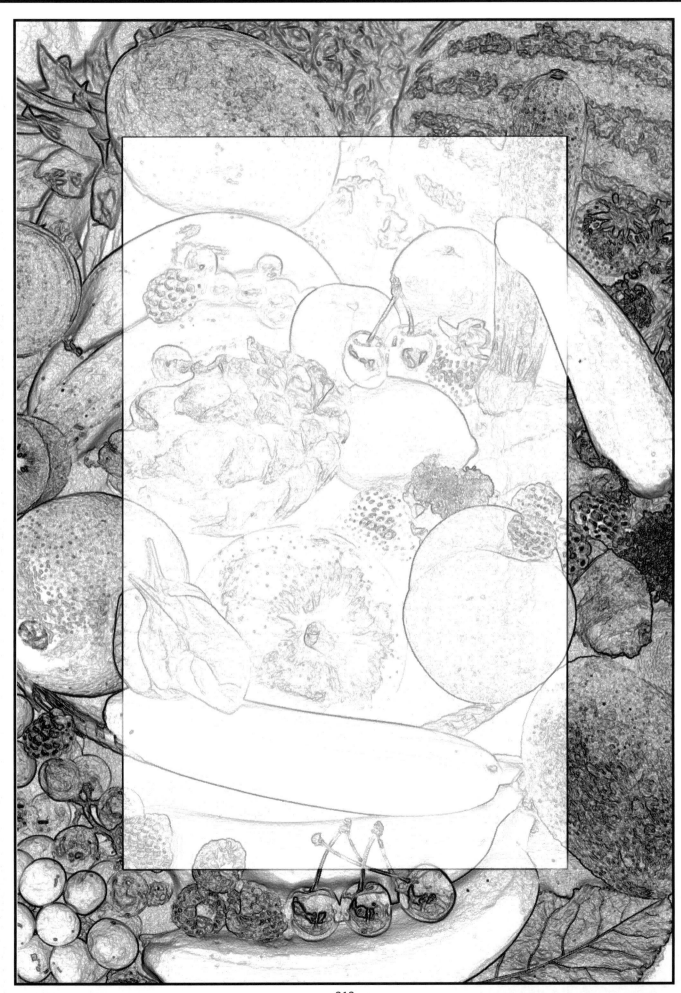

QUESTIONS & ANALYSIS (Q&A):

How did you like this Shake?

_____

_____

Describe the flavor, consistency, color and texture:

_____

_____

_____

How would you improve this recipe?

_____

_____

_____

How would make this recipe sweeter, or less sweet?

_____

_____

_____

How would you make this recipe without dairy?

_____

_____

_____

PEANUT BUTTER PERFECTION!

How and where are peanuts commonly grown?
What is the climate like?

_____

_____

_____

_____

How is peanut butter made and who invented it? When and why
was it invented?

_____

_____

_____

_____

Find a recipe to make your own peanut butter and write it out.

_____

_____

_____

_____

DRAW A PICTURE OF A PEANUT INSIDE AND OUTSIDE THE SHELL.

List some nutrition facts about peanut butter.

_____

_____

_____

_____

List some different uses for peanut shells.

_____

_____

_____

_____

THREE CHEERS FOR CHOCOLATE!

How well do you know it?

All over the world, people can't seem to get enough chocolate. But do you know where it originally came from? Write a brief history.

_____

_____

_____

_____

There is a specific process to turn the Cacao bean into nibs that can be used to produce the chocolate the we so love, describe it.

_____

_____

_____

_____

What is your favorite kind of chocolate? Do a little research on your brand, describe the production process from tree to your table.

_____

_____

_____

_____

ILLUSTRATE CACAO GROWING.

List some nutrition facts about chocolate & dark chocolate.

_____

_____

_____

_____

Find a recipe that uses chocolate as a main ingredient and write it out.

_____

_____

_____

_____

More Fun Activities...

1. Create your own smoothie recipe using any of the following ingredients, feel free to add ingredients not listed. (Make sure to measure, write down your recipe and give it a fun title).

CARROT	LEMON
STRAWBERRY	COCONUT MILK
RASPBERRY	PINEAPPLE JUICE
SPINACH	PROTEIN POWDER

2. CREATIVE WRITING

Choose a favorite smoothie you made. Write a short story, about how all the ingredients, went on a journey, and became a smoothie.

_____

_____

_____

_____

_____

_____

_____

_____

_____

_____

ILLUSTRATE YOUR STORY.

3. POETRY

EXPRESS YOUR POETIC SIDE:

Choose a recipe that you LIKED, and one you did NOT LIKE, and write TWO different HAIKU POEMS.

What is a HAIKU POEM and how do you write one? (Do your research.)

> Here is an example of a
> HAIKU POEM inspired by the:
> CHOCOLATE BANANA NUT
> Smoothie (with added honey)

NANA NANA NUT (5 syllables)

HONEY BUZZING BUMBLE BEE (7 syllables)

MILKY SILKY SWEET (5 syllables)

Use the next page to write and illustrate your Haiku poems.

4. SCIENCE:

Once you have consumed your delicious smoothie, describe WHAT HAPPENS NEXT.

Do some research. Write about how the DIGESTIVE SYSTEM works in the human body.

ILLUSTRATE DIGESTION:

5. MATH

Suppose you were having a **BIRTHDAY PARTY**,

and you had 7 friends come over.

They all want your **FAMOUS SMOOTHIE!**

DOES YOUR FAVORITE RECIPE MAKE ENOUGH SMOOTHIE FOR 7 FRIENDS AND YOURSELF?

Most likely not, figure out how much more you will need

to increase your smoothie recipe, double? Triple?

6. MONEY MATH

WRITE A SMOOTHIE RECIPE BELOW & NOTE THE COST OF EACH ITEM.

ITEM:	COST:

HOW MUCH DOES IT COST TO MAKE ONE SMOOTHIE?

IT'S SMOOTHIE MAKING TIME

CREATE YOUR OWN RECIPE!

7. NUTRITION

If you were to LOOK AT all the ingredients you now know about, and some of the NUTRITION FACTS. What would be a good smoothie to make if someone wanted MORE BRAIN POWER?

HINT: Research antioxidants and brainy foods.

Write the recipe here.

❄

SEARCH AND FIND MORE "BRAIN POWER" INGREDIENTS. LIST THEM BELOW.

8. SEEDS

Seeds are interesting, they can be found in many forms. Whole, raw or roasted, with or without salt, ground into flour, even pressed into oils .

Start with FLAX SEED. Below are 3 sample questions. On the next page pick two more seeds to answer these same questions in the space provided.

Which form of (flax) seed is easiest for the body to digest and absorb nutrients?

What kind of nutrients are in (flax) seed?

What seems to be the most important reason that people add (flax) seed to their diet?

DRAW AND LABEL EACH SEED

9. DEFINE AND DISCUSS:

ORGANIC:

_____
_____
_____
_____

GMO:

_____
_____
_____
_____

GMO-FREE:

_____
_____
_____

CONVENTIONAL FARMING:

_____
_____
_____
_____

WHAT KIND OF FARMING DO YOU THINK IS BEST?

_____

_____

_____

_____

WRITE A LIST OF COUNTRIES THAT HAVE BANNED GMO FARMING.

_____

_____

_____

_____

_____

_____

_____

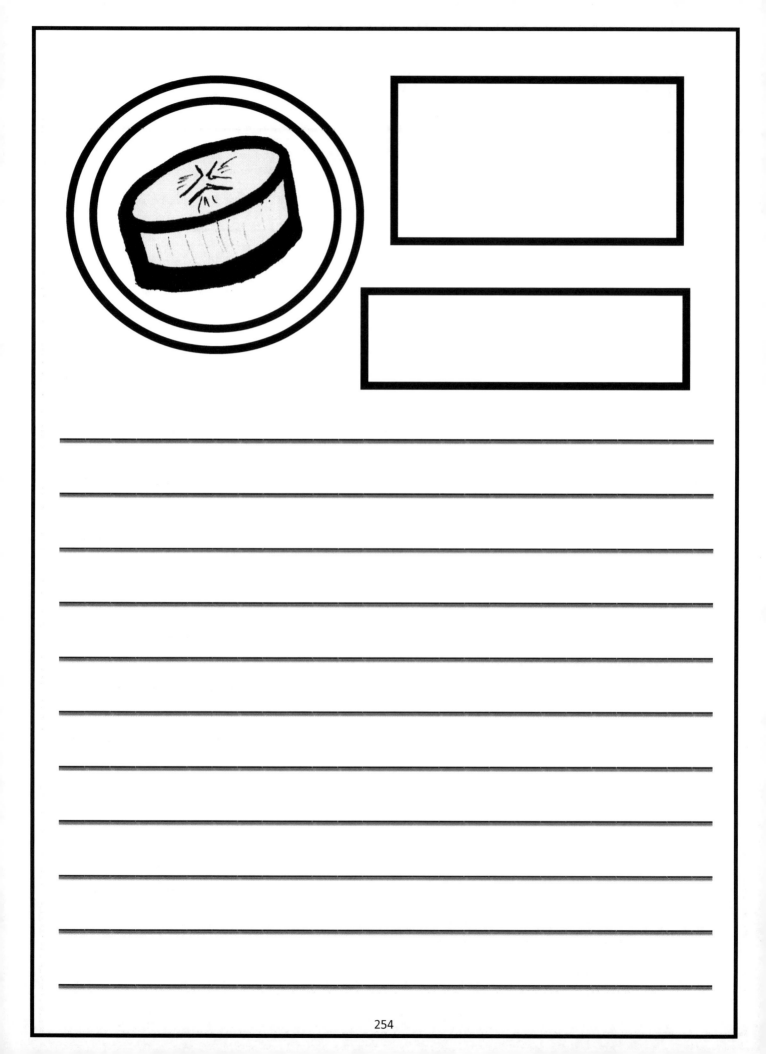

10. RESEARCH: EARLY AMERICAN FARMS.

HOW DID THE NATIVE AMERICANS PLANT THEIR CROPS? PIONEERS? AMISH?

_____

_____

_____

_____

_____

_____

_____

_____

_____

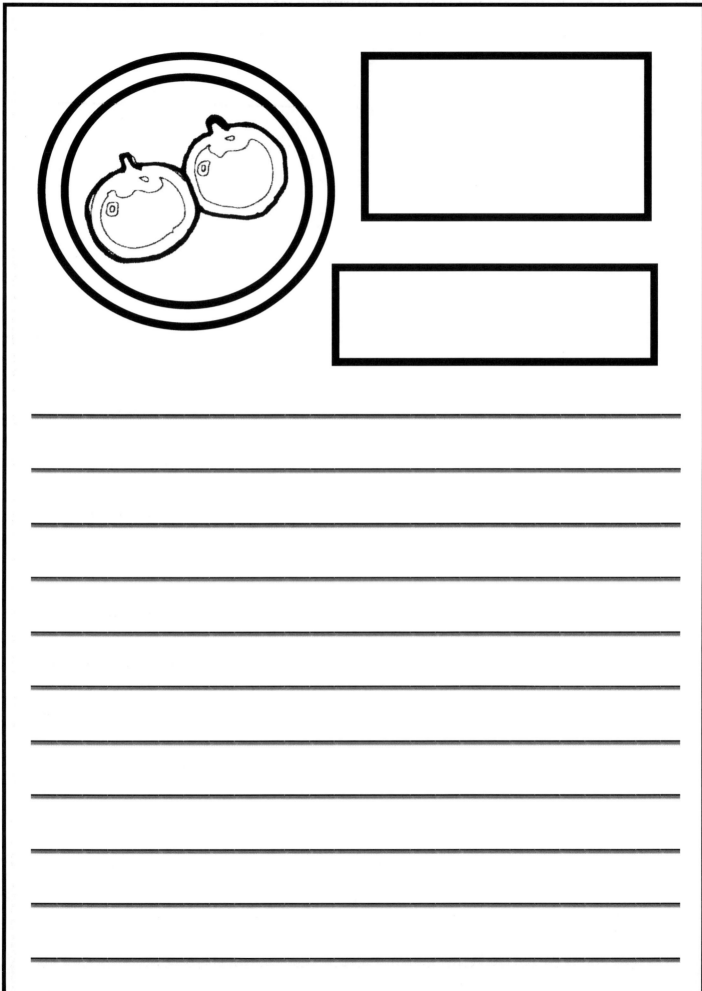

II. VIDEO RESEARCH

1. Watch a smoothie making video, take notes. Try to duplicate their recipe.

2. Pick an ingredient used in this book, watch a cooking show/video that uses it. Write out the recipe and try it at home.

3. Watch a travel documentary about a place you came across in this book. Draw a map.

4. Get to know your world. Find different videos about farming/growing food on each continent. Take notes, draw maps.

12. PLAN A GARDEN

What do people commonly plant in your area?

_____

_____

What do you want to grow? What can you grow?

_____

_____

Will you plant an outdoor or window garden?

_____

_____

Where will you get supplies? Estimate the cost?

_____

_____

MAP OUT YOUR GARDEN:

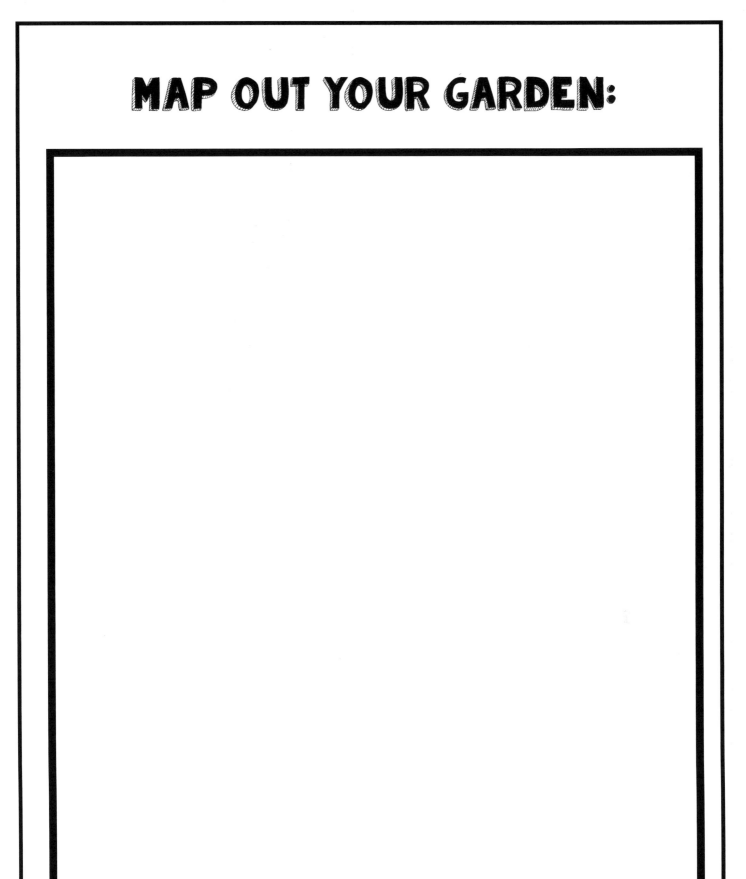

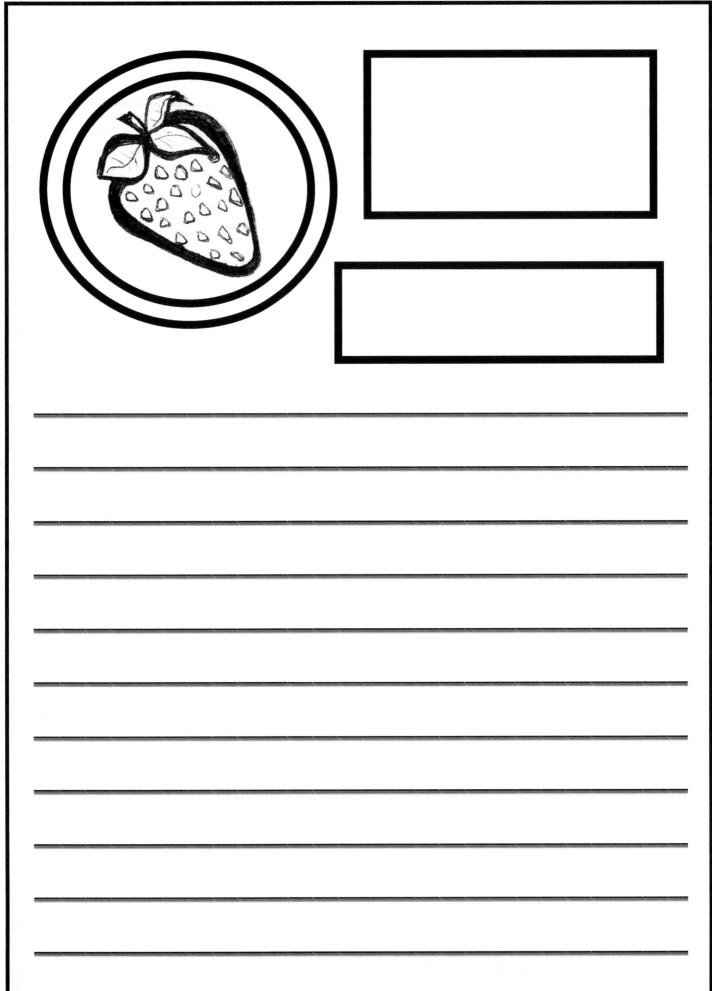

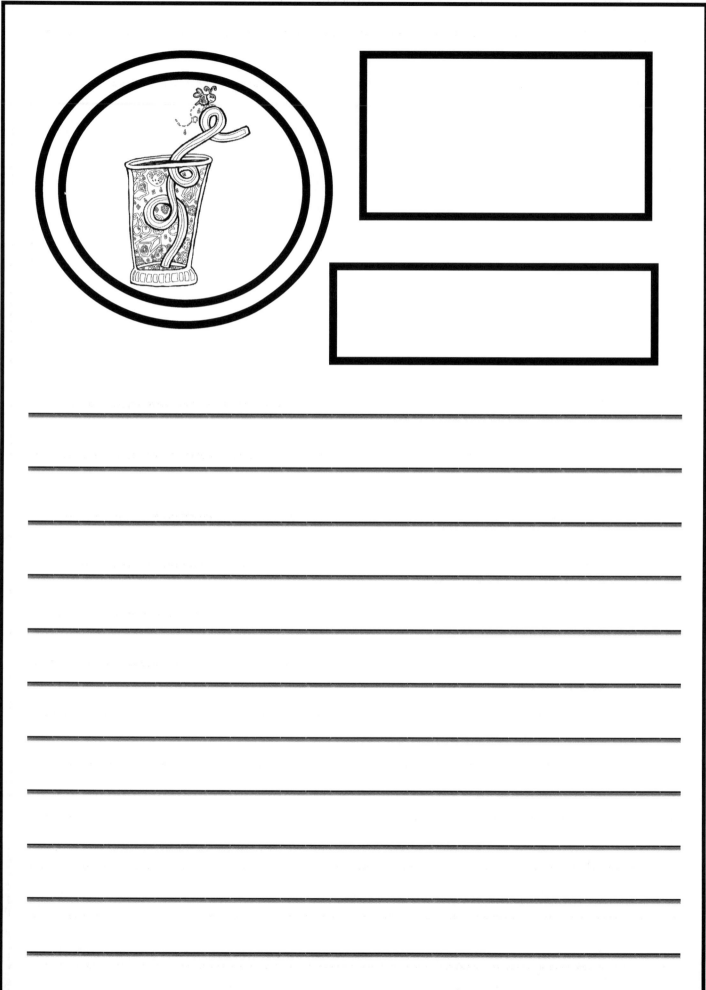

Made in the USA
Columbia, SC
07 December 2017